Anti-Catholic Myths Debunked

ARCHBISHOP PATRICK JOHN RYAN

ANTI-CATHOLIC MYTHS DEBUNKED

Five Common Misconceptions
Answered and Explained

SOPHIA INSTITUTE PRESS
Manchester, New Hampshire

Sophia Institute Press
Box 5284, Manchester, NH 03108
1-800-888-9344

www.SophiaInstitute.com

Sophia Institute Press® is a registered trademark of Sophia Institute.

Library of Congress Cataloging-in-Publication Data

Names: Ryan, P. J. (Patrick John), 1831-1911, author.
Title: Anti-Catholic myths debunked : five common misconceptions answered and explained / Right Reverend Patrick John Ryan.
Other titles: What Catholics do not believe
Description: Manchester, New Hampshire : Sophia Institute Press, 2016. |
   Originally published under title: What Catholics do not believe : St.
   Louis : P. Fox, 1878. | Includes bibliographical references.
Identifiers: LCCN 2016039471 | ISBN 9781622823567 (pbk. : alk. paper)
Subjects: LCSH: Catholic Church—Doctrines.
Classification: LCC BX1755 .R9 2016 | DDC 282—dc23 LC record available at https://lccn.loc.gov/2016039471

First printing

Contents

Editor's Note

The following pages are drawn from a lecture that Archbishop Ryan gave in St. Louis on December 16, 1877. They have been edited slightly to eliminate anachronisms and other anomalies. Where possible, we have identified persons mentioned by the archbishop and sources of the quotations he cites.

Anti-Catholic Myths Debunked

Introduction

✠

The primary object of this book is to remove certain prejudices against the Church—prejudices rooted not in what Catholics believe, but in what we *do not* believe.

The positive side of the question—what we *do really believe* on these points—will be found stated in nearly every instance and implied in all. I did not think it essential to state all the reasons for the positive side, because the statement of the *fact* that we do not believe certain doctrines is the chief point in view.

As to the reason for this topic, I had promised to deliver a discourse in aid of a pressing parochial object—the payment of the indebtedness on our new school building—and I had determined on the subject I should select, when I was somewhat surprised by an invitation from the Reverend Doctor Snyder, pastor of the Unitarian church in this city, to deliver in his church on a Sunday evening a lecture on "The Claims of the Catholic Church."

This confirmed my resolution as to the subject but somewhat changed my mode of treating it. The Reverend Doctor assured me of the presence of a large audience of Protestants, many of whom, he stated, were ignorant of Catholicism, except as defined by its enemies and slanderers.

I could not resist the impulse to address such an audience and defend what is as dear to me as my very existence — the Catholic Church. Although I could not accept the pastor's invitation to lecture in his church, I hoped that non-Catholics would not object to meet me on neutral ground — Mercantile Library Hall. I was not mistaken. The pastor and many of his people attended, and a morning paper states that half of the large audience was Protestant.

I hope I said nothing that could pain them. It is not, and never was, in my heart to do so, in discussing religious questions with outsiders. Without compromising a single iota of truth, we can, like Jesus, be at once kind and true.

As to the lecture itself, although I had delivered the substance of it before, I had never written it all out as the topics were as familiar to me as they are to every Catholic clergyman. Even now I must depend, in parts of it, on a corrected stenographic report, as it is expedient not to delay publication. Hence the haste and redundancy of extempore speaking will occasionally be detected.

I send it forth, however, with the hope that God may bless it on its way and that, for some soul in darkness, it may at least help to remove the impediments to light—lending a hand, as it were, in rolling back the stone that closes the sepulcher, so that, hearing the omnipotent voice of grace, the soul may, like the brother of Mary and Martha, come out into the life and light and liberty of the Truth that alone "can make her free."[1]

St. Louis
Feast of St. John the Evangelist
December 27, 1877

[1] See John 8:32.

Five Charges against the Church

✠

I propose to expound on the subject of what Catholics *do not* believe. That is, as no doubt you already anticipate, I propose to correct some erroneous impressions with regard to important points of Catholic doctrine. After long discussion with non-Catholics of various religious denominations and many of no denomination at all, I am profoundly impressed with the conviction that most of the opposition to the Catholic Church and the gravest obstacle to that mutual good feeling that ought to exist among members of all religious organizations, and, indeed, among all men, arise chiefly from a misunderstanding of what Catholic doctrines on important points really are.

Explanations of these doctrines seem almost as necessary these days as in the days of the apologies of the Early Fathers, some of them written seventeen hundred years ago.

My relations with non-Catholics have taught me also, strange as you may think it, a great respect for what are called bigoted people. They are generally people deeply in earnest, people who hate injustice and deceit, and because they imagine — falsely — that the Catholic Church is a marvelous combination of the powers of both, they detest it. They also form very often the most fervent and the most persevering converts to the Church.

We can scarcely be angry with them, because they are angry with an institution of impossible existence. Their idea of the Catholic Church would be a combination of contradictions. They are opposed not to the Catholic Church but to something that they think is the Church.

To disabuse them of these errors, to teach these honest, upright, devoted, and religious people, in their way, what we believe, to remove these misapprehensions, is one of the duties before me.

It is a subject that ought to be interesting to a great number of people. First, it should be interesting as a matter, indeed, of justice, to those who protest against the Church. No man has a right to protest against the opinions of another man until he shall have known these opinions from the man who holds them or from the organization that professes them.

This is very apparent in politics, by which it may be illustrated. Suppose a man, a stranger in the country, who knows but little of politics, has associated chiefly with Republicans. Suppose he meets a Democrat and protests against the doctrine of the Democrat, and the Democrat asks him: "Sir, have you ever read an authorized exposition of what the Democrats believe?"

"No, sir."

"Have you ever heard a speech of a Democratic orator or representative man — one who is authorized to expound the principles of our party?"

"No, sir."

"Have you ever had an exhaustive private conversation on the subject of the principles of the Democratic Party?"

"Well, I don't know that I have."

"What have you heard about it?"

"I confess, on reflection, that what I have heard of you has been from Republicans."

"Well, sir," says the Democrat, "they are a very bad authority. You have to know Democracy from Democrats."

And, on the same principle, you have to know Catholicism from Catholics.

It is impossible, then, to know what men believe unless they themselves, or someone authorized by them, explain their doctrines. Hence it is a matter of justice that those who protest against us should know from us what we believe.

And the subject is of interest for another reason: the tide of infidelity is sweeping onward. The members of religious organizations outside the pale of the Roman Catholic Church are obliged necessarily from their principles to endeavor to stem this tide of infidelity. And now here is that Church, here are hundreds of millions banded together under one head, fighting a similar battle against infidelity.

Can they be ignored by the divided and still dividing societies outside the pale of this Church?

Can these bodies expect to overcome infidelity, independently of any aid indirectly given, if you please, by this great organization?

Therefore those who are interested in the truth of the Christian religion ought to understand something of the doctrine of the largest, most powerful, and most united organization that opposes the infidelity of the day.

"But," someone may say, "the Catholic Church is not worth examining. She can be but of little aid in the battle against the wrong. The Church is on her dying bed; her energies are paralyzed; she has lost her grasp upon the nations of Europe, where she ruled supremely, and she cannot grasp the younger or more energetic nations that are too progressive and aggressive to admit her doctrine, or to bow under her sway.

"Therefore, she is only as an institution of the past, without the vitality that is necessary to sustain her in the future. She can be but of little aid. She has stood like the statue in the vision of the Babylonian king. She has stood like that mighty colossus of gold, silver, brass and iron, but whose feet were of clay and iron mixed, and young progress — religious and scientific — like a fragment of rock, has struck this proud colossus. It is swaying to and fro; it shall fall, and great shall be the fall thereof, and nothing shall be left but the pulverized fragments of the colossal institution."[2]

Thus do they think who believe the Church's day is over.

Yet one day the Church is said to be dying, and the next day we find her giving audiences to the nations. We find in her an interest and a vitality; we find her gathering audiences that want to know something about this institution, so wonderful — dying, and yet overcoming obstacles that no institution that ever existed overcame; an institution of which Lord Macaulay says, "There is not, and there never was, on this earth an institution of human policy so deserving of examination as the Roman Catholic Church."[3]

[2] See Dan. 2:31–35.

[3] Thomas Babington, Lord Macaulay (1800–1859), *Critical and Historical Essays Contributed to the Edinburgh Review*, 6th ed., 3 vols. (London: Longman, Brown, Green, and Longmans, 1849), 401.

Again, is it of interest to the infidel, the skeptic, the rationalist, or by whatever name he may be known, that he should understand something concerning what *are not* the doctrines of this Church, and by implication *what are*?

There are honest infidels as well as honest Protestants. From a defect in religious education and sometimes from an injudicious overeducation in religion; from want of judgment, and in early youth overrestraint of the mind, and a rigorism that rendered religion unamiable; and from various other causes, they have been influenced to cast aside a belief in revelation.

Yet this class of persons — and I think I know something of them — are not all settled in mind. The religious element is in every human heart. These men and women are anxious. They talk about religion. Sometimes they may even persecute religion, but they are far from being at peace themselves. They must talk about it. There is something that impels them, simply because the religious element is there and must be satisfied.

Now, there is a large class of these infidels, skeptics, or rationalists, by whatever name they may be called, who have come to the conclusion that, if God gave a revelation to man, if there be a historic church in existence, that church is the Catholic Church. The question with them is "Rome or reason?"

If there is no revelation, then they are rational, they think. They keep apart and profess to act out, as far as they can, the knowledge that they have of right and wrong in the natural order.

But there are some really conscientious Protestants who would prefer that this agnostic body of men should be Christians and Roman Catholics than that they should remain infidels and rejecters of revelation, as I myself would prefer a member of some religious denomination, possessing at least some of the truths of Christianity (for even a human faith in any single doctrine is of advantage) to an utter unbeliever in all God's revelation. Therefore, these Protestants ought to be interested in these unbelievers' understanding of what Catholics really hold. Yet some are afraid to examine the Church lest it should prove to be true.

I remember one of them—an illustrious man— the late Dr. Brownson,[4] who told me more than

---

[4] Orestes Brownson (1803–1876).

twenty years ago, when I expressed my surprise that he had been so long a time in coming into the Church, "For years before I became a Catholic, when I was more of an infidel than anything else, I had the thought that the truth might be the Church; but I was afraid to touch it, for I would prefer almost to risk my immortal soul than to become a papist in Boston at that time."

There is another class of men who would gladly embrace the truth if they knew it, as Dr. Brownson finally did; a class of men who say: "We cannot enter into that Church and save the dignity of our manhood; we cannot accept, with the intelligence God gave us, these dogmas. How can we, without giving up all claim to consistency, accept what appears to us utterly irrational?"

Perhaps, gentlemen, what appears to you absurd is not what Catholics believe, but what Catholics *do not* believe.

Let us examine together some of these doctrines. Let us see whether the obstacles to your approaching this Church are not founded on a misconception of what she really believes. Let us see whether it cannot be a question, not of Rome *or* reason, but of Rome *and* reason.

Again, independently of all religious considerations, a man who desires to understand the philosophy of history must know something of the real doctrines of the Church. For the Church has had more to do with humanity, has had more effect on human society than any organization in existence—or that has been in existence—since the time of our divine Lord.

Therefore, to understand the history of our race, to trace effects to their causes, it is necessary that we should understand this Church, understand something of the real doctrines that she professes, because the influence that she exercised is an influence arising logically from these very doctrines and cannot be understood by those who do not understand the doctrines themselves.

Guizot, the French statesman, and, as you are aware, a Protestant, speaking on this subject, says:

> The Church has exercised a vast and important influence upon the moral and intellectual order of Europe, upon the notions, sentiments, and manners of society. This fact is evident.

The intellectual and moral progress of Europe has been essentially theological. Look at its history from the fifth to the sixteenth century, and you will find throughout that theology has possessed and directed the human mind. Every idea is impressed with theology. Every question that has been started, whether philosophical, political, or historical, has been considered from a religious point of view....

We shall find that the same fact holds if we travel through the regions of literature; the habits, the sentiments, the language of theology there show themselves at every step.

This influence, taken altogether, has been salutary. It not only kept up and ministered to the intellectual movement in Europe, but the system of doctrines and precepts by whose authority it stamped its impress upon that movement was incalculably superior to any which the ancient world had known....

Notwithstanding all the evil, all the abuses which may have crept into the Church; notwithstanding all the acts of tyranny of which she has been guilty, we must still acknowledge her influence upon the progress and culture of the human race to have been beneficial, and that she has assisted in its development rather than its compression, in its expansion rather than its confinement.[5]

So to understand the philosophy of history, we must know something of this Church and of the theology that had such influence, as Guizot says, upon the direction of affairs in Europe through so many ages.

Such are some of the reasons why this lecture ought to interest different classes of inquirers.

Now I come to the lecture itself.

In order to render it, perhaps, more interesting and clear, I shall have it take the form of an indictment against the Catholic Church, in the first place bringing forward the counts of that indictment, and

---

[5] François Pierre Guillaume Guizot (1787–1874), *General History of Civilization in Europe: From the Fall of the Roman Empire to the French Revolution*, 2nd American ed. (New York: D. Appleton, 1840), 179–181.

in the second place, showing that the charges in this indictment are founded upon what Catholics *do not* believe, and therefore the indictment must fall to the ground.

ACCUSATION 1

Church authority enslaves human reason.

✠

Placing myself in the position of an objector, I would first say, "I charge the Catholic Church with having enslaved the human intellect, with having degraded religion, with having demoralized the individual and public conscience."

She enslaves the human intellect by her doctrinal authority. Man, endowed by Almighty God with reason, is forced by the Church to submit that reason to the dictate of a human institution, and although he may, with that reason, already have come to a certain conclusion, the moment this Church authority speaks, he must bow his head and submit to it notwithstanding his previous convictions.

Imagine an intellectual balance before you. A man deliberates on a certain question. He puts the arguments for the doctrine into one scale and the arguments against it into the other. Following his reason, he comes to a conclusion averse to the doctrine, and the scale against the doctrine sinks, and the scale with

Catholics surrender their will to the pope
(nineteenth-century anti-Catholic cartoon)

the arguments for it rises. Now, using the reason that God gave him, he has come to this conclusion.

Then he hears of a decision of Church authority — the pope speaking *ex cathedra* or a decree of a general council. That man, in opposition to his previous convictions — must submit his intellect.

The Church, as it were, has rudely pulled down the lighter scale, and he must bow and cry *Credo!* Here, it may be urged, is an enslaving of the human intellect.

Priest fends off the Bible
(nineteenth-century anti-Catholic cartoon)

ACCUSATION 2

The Church withholds the Bible from Catholics.

Again, the intellect is enslaved, because the Church takes from it the grounds on which it can form an intelligent judgment: she takes the Scriptures of God from man, or, if she permits him to read them, it must be with her own interpretation. Here, therefore, is slavery of the intellect of the very worst character.

ACCUSATION 3

The Church blindfolds reason with art, music, and sentimentalism.

---✠---

And again, by her gorgeous ceremonial, by her use of the arts—architecture, sculpture, music, painting, and poetry—she cheats, as it were, reason.

Reason has to be silent, and the Catholic, over-awed by the majesty and magnitude of her grand cathedrals, dazzled by the excessive light and glory and by her use of the fine arts—the Catholic led captive, a willing captive, if you please, by her love of the beautiful, her sentimentalism—is no longer reasonable. He is the slave of this sentimentalism.

It is said of a man, who, being present in St. Peter's Church in Rome amid all the splendor of some grand ceremonial, found himself kneeling on the marble pavement, that he felt his heart moved as it had never been moved before. The religious aesthetic influence was upon him, but he rose superior to it and said: "This is not reason: this is sentiment; this is imagination. I will break these enchanting bonds; I will be a man and follow my reason alone."

Lavish Corpus Christi Procession in 1830

ACCUSATION 4

The Church wrongly promotes love of Mary and the saints.

Again, it is urged that the Church degrades religion because the great object of religion is God, and any power that places on his throne any being but God, and offers that creature worship, is degrading religion, because it is degrading the object of all religion.

And yet the Church, by her devotion to the Blessed Virgin, to saints and angels, by her devotion to even inanimate objects — pictures, statues, relics, and so forth — substitutes something that is not God for religious worship and therefore degrades religion.

Sistine Madonna by Raphael

ACCUSATION 5

Catholic priests perform deeds reserved for God alone.

✠

Finally, she demoralizes the individual and the public conscience, because she teaches the doctrine that a man may hold the place of God; a man may be the judge of the conscience of another; a man may forgive sins as he pleases; and because of this fatal facility of forgiving, the horror for sin must be lessened.

A culprit goes to this tribunal and has forgiveness extended to him and goes away and sins again, again to be forgiven! Here is a man, like himself, a sinner, who has this tremendous power to forgive sins as he pleases.

Hence, the individual conscience must be demoralized, and the nation, which is but a collection of individuals, must become demoralized; and hence the low and corrupt condition of so many Catholic peoples.

Confession

Honest Answers to These False Charges

✣

I have brought forward these objections — having placed myself for a moment in the position of an adversary of the Church — and I have endeavored to do so honestly and as strongly, I think, as could be expected from a man not accustomed to anti-Catholic public speaking.

But feeling that there is a power to answer them, feeling that the truth can never suffer in this conflict with error because *these accusations all concern what Catholics do not believe*, I have put them as strongly as it is possible for me to do, and I proceed now to reply to these charges.

Do not fear that I will employ tricks in my defense of the Church. Yes, it is true that almost anything can be plausibly defended — that objections can be ingeniously explained away. (A man has written a defense even of Judas Iscariot!)

I have been told of a case of special pleading, or rather special judging, by explaining away of charges, that occurred in this state and is an amusing illustration of what I have been speaking about.

An old Democratic judge found himself in the awkward position of being called to try two clergymen who, during the time that the test oath[6] was in force here, had been guilty of the high crime of preaching the gospel without taking the "iron-clad oath."

He asked the first preacher arraigned before him to what religious denomination he belonged, and the clergyman replied, "I am a member of the Christian Church or what is called sometimes by outsiders the Campbellite Church."

---

[6] Immediately after the Civil War, officials as well as preachers in Missouri and many other states were required, as a condition of office, to swear that they had never in any way supported the Confederacy.

"Oh," said the old Democratic judge, "I knew Alexander Campbell myself. I am a Baptist. I understand the doctrines of your sect. Now, I don't call preaching the gospel according to Alexander Campbell *preaching the gospel at all*, and therefore you don't come under this law."

The next clergyman was a Baptist of the same shade as the judge himself. The old man asked for the witness against this clergyman, and when he was produced, he said to him: "How does this reverend gentleman preach?"

"Well," replied the witness, "as I am on my oath, I must say that he is the worst preacher I ever heard. I would not call that preaching at all. I would call that *trying to preach*."

"Well," said the judge, "this law declares a man guilty who preaches, but not a man who only *tries* to preach; therefore, sir, you can continue to try to preach, but you must be very careful not to preach the gospel without taking the oath."

Special pleading, explaining away, defending when the prejudices are in favor of the person defended: in all this there may be, indeed, much delusion, but it is impossible that you should be deceived by any explaining away in answer to the indictments that I have just brought against the Catholic Church because her doctrines are not variable opinions; they are sharply and authoritatively defined and are easily known.

Were I to tell you of any one doctrine that I asserted Catholics do not believe, but which they do, there is not a child in this city who has learned his catechism who could not afterward detect the fraud. Hence, as these doctrines are the same everywhere, as you can find them in every authorized exposition of what Catholics really believe, there is no fear of special pleading or misrepresentation. Therefore, I will at once proceed to examine the subject, and to defend, by stating what Catholics *do not believe* about these several points.

Church authority does not enslave human reason.

In the first place, Catholics do not believe that they are bound to submit their intellects to the decision of a human institution. They have first convinced themselves that the Church to which they pay allegiance and by which they are taught the truths of revelation is a *divine* institution, that she is an unerring messenger from God to them. Therefore, if they submit to a decision of the Church, they submit to a decision of a tribunal that their own reason has already accepted as an unerring tribunal.

If they were obliged to receive the decision on matters of faith without having already been convinced that this decision came from a tribunal that could not err, then they would be slaves; but they have a reason for submitting their reason. There is no possibility of slavery in this case.

There is, on the contrary, a respect for the real dignity and liberty of human reason. Having come to a certain conviction on a certain point, I will never abandon the reason that God gave me, except to the decision of a tribunal that my reason has already accepted as unerring.

The man holds the balance in his hand. The scale against the doctrine descends; the other ascends.

Now comes new evidence that he did not have before when he weighed the arguments: he learns of a decision by a tribunal that his reason has previously accepted as unerring. This is *new* evidence that he places on the side of the scale that was lighter before. This new evidence weighs down that side, and bowing his head—his intelligence also bowing—the man says, "Credo" (I believe). His reason accepts it; he is no slave in this decision.

Dearer to me and to every person, dearer than was Isaac to Abraham, is his reason. It is what makes a man all that he is. Abraham would have erred grievously if he had offered his son on the mountain if he were not absolutely certain of God's stern behest. He never could have offered to sacrifice that son on a probability that God required it. He never could have offered to sacrifice that son on a message received from Almighty God unless, indeed, that messenger was rendered unerring by Almighty God. But having received the order and having been certain of that order, then he prepares to offer his son.

So with my reason.

I will offer it only on the mountain of God. I will offer it only at God's behest, and even then I have only to offer it, not to sacrifice it. Reason, like Isaac, is offered, but, like Isaac, it is not sacrificed, because there comes a reason for giving up my reason at the time. There comes this decision of this unerring tribunal.

Therefore, in any case where the Church is unerring, the dignity of human reason is preserved. The dignity of human reason is preserved here when a man is certain he hears the command of Almighty God and hears it through a messenger who cannot deliver a false report.

The Church does not withhold the Bible from Catholics.

It is not true that the Church enslaves reason by keeping from it the means of forming a judgment. She does not hide the Scriptures from the people; she was the guardian of the Scriptures from the beginning. Her monks of old industriously translated them. To them, humanly speaking, we owe their preservation, as we owe the preservation of the classics. The Church is their guardian. She does not and never did forbid the people to read the Word of God.

Yes, she condemns spurious editions of the Scriptures. She has to protect those oracles of God from corruption, but never did she hide them from the people.

On the contrary, that she recommends her children to read them is evident, as you will see in many of the Catholic Bibles for sale in our bookstores. In every Catholic bookstore there are many editions of the Bible of various sizes and prices; in them are recommendations to study them, and in many of those Bibles there is a letter from Pope Pius VI, to the most reverend Anthony Martini, Archbishop of Florence, on his translation of the Holy Bible into Italian. The pope says:

> Beloved son, at a time when a vast number of books which most grossly attack the Catholic religion are circulated, even among the unlearned, to the great danger of souls, you judge exceedingly well that the faithful should be excited to the reading of the Holy Scriptures; for these are the most abundant sources which ought to be left open to everyone to draw from them purity of morals and of doctrine, to eradicate the errors which are so widely disseminated in these corrupt times.

So there is clearly no prohibition on the part of any Church authority, that the people should read these oracles of Almighty God.

The Church interprets what needs interpretation for her people. Does that lessen the dignity of the Scriptures? Does that enslave the intellect?

The Scriptures themselves tell us that in them there are things "hard to understand, which the ignorant and unstable twist to their own destruction."[7] Hence, as there are difficulties in them, and as they need an interpreter of those difficulties, this interpreter is given.

Are the laws of Missouri degraded because there is a supreme court to interpret them? Does the fact that there are judges to interpret prevent the people from reading the laws?

Does the fact that there are judges to interpret lessen the dignity of the people — lessen the sanction of the laws? No. And so there is no injustice done to the Catholic intellect in providing what every state in the world has provided, in order to have unity in that state — someone to interpret the laws.

[7] 2 Peter 3:16, RSV.

Hence it is false that the Church enslaves the human intellect by taking from it the means of discovering the truth, for she recommends these divine oracles — for she preserved these divine oracles — and she interprets them, being constituted to do so by Him who said:

> "Going therefore, teach ye all nations ... to observe all things whatsoever I have commanded you: and behold I am with you all days, even to the consummation of the world."[8]

> "As the Father hath sent me, I also send you."[9]

> "All power is given to me in heaven and in earth."[10]

> "He that heareth you, heareth me."[11]

> "If he will not hear the church, let him be to thee as the heathen and publican."[12]

[8] Matt. 28:19–20.
[9] John 20:21.
[10] Matt. 28:18.
[11] Luke 10:16.
[12] Matt. 18:17.

Now, He did not remain with those twelve men as individuals but as a corporate body, which He constituted as the supreme court in spiritual matters to interpret His law and to decide disputes.

He spoke to those men themselves, of their own deaths in the future; and yet He said, "I am with you always, to the close of the age."

In the United States Congress, when one man dies, another takes his place, and the powers given to the original Congress are retained by the Congress of today, although there is not one man of the members of that original Congress alive.

So it was in the apostolic college: when one died, another took his place. When Judas prevaricated and killed himself, Matthias was elected, and Matthias was as much an apostle as Judas had been. When another died, another took his place, so that the apostolic body still remains until today, unshorn of a single apostolic power; it remains to judge, to interpret, to decide disputes.

Almighty God provided the Jewish people with a tribunal to settle disputes that should arise among them; a tribunal or supreme court for deciding the interpretation of His law.[13] In Deuteronomy, they were ordered to go to the high priest when there was a dispute concerning the meaning of the law, and when the high priest decided it, it was death to contradict his decision. So they had their supreme court.

Shall it be said that Christianity is worse off than Judaism? Shall it be said that there is no authority left on this earth to settle a man's doubts and difficulties?

The Jews had it. Plato asked for it when he said that a man could never be certain on religious questions until God Himself would speak. God, or someone whom Almighty God would preserve from error in teaching, must speak; and therefore there is constituted in the Catholic Church this supreme deciding power—a supreme court in spiritual matters.

Hence the unity of the Church; hence the power of the Church; hence that marvelous combination of the most discordant elements; hence the men from north and south and east and west, of every tribe and tongue and people—hundreds of millions believing

[13] Although they possessed the Scriptures, these were not deemed all sufficient.

in every iota the same truths, because when there was a question of doubt, there was left an authority to decide; and, as there would be anarchy in the state of Missouri in a month if the supreme court were abolished,[14] so there is anarchy in the various organizations outside the Catholic Church, dividing and subdividing; essentially so, because the very principle of union, the deciding power, is wanting.

That power exists in the Catholic Church; therefore, in the young and energetic nations, in spite of all the opposition and misrepresentation, she is gradually gaining hold upon them, and no amount of scientific investigation and no reformation or changes in religion — nothing, can shake the united force of that marvelous organization, united by this supreme deciding power.

[14] The secular and spiritual supreme tribunals are alike in this: they are essential to unity — each in its order. They differ in this: the spiritual court, deciding for the mind itself in matters of faith, must be infallible to be final. "What supremacy is to the temporal, infallibility is to the spiritual order" (Joseph de Maistre).

The Church does not blindfold reason with art, music, and sentimentalism.

Neither can it be said that this Church enslaves the human intellect by her magnificent ceremonial and her use of the arts in the worship of Almighty God, because Catholics do not believe that religion consists in external pomp and show of ceremony.

We must worship God "in spirit and in truth"[15] or there is no religion. The pomp of ceremony, the use of the arts: these things may aid man in worshipping in spirit and in truth, but without this, worship is

[15] John 4:24.

magnificent pageantry, if you please, but pageantry nonetheless.

Now, the object of the use of the ceremonial, the object of the use of the arts in the worship of God, is to aid man to worship in spirit and in truth. First of all, we use these things as a suitable expression of the soul's allegiance to Almighty God. Some of the ceremonies of the Catholic Church are not seen by the people at all. In the consecration of a Church, during part of the ceremony, the people are not even admitted.

The Church performs her ceremonies primarily for the Divine Eye. You behold the priest, for instance, in the Holy Sacrifice of the Mass, turned away from the people, speaking in a tongue unknown to them, and in a tone to them inaudible.[16]

As regards the art of architecture, Pugin, the great English architect,[17] tells us that he noticed in the old English cathedrals of Catholic days that the portions of these buildings hidden away from

---

[16] Here Bishop Ryan is alluding to the pre–Vatican II Mass, which was offered in Latin.

[17] Augustus Welby Northmore Pugin (1812–1852)

the people were as elaborately finished as the most conspicuous parts. These men built for the Divine Presence, but these ceremonies and these arts were destined, also, to touch the human heart and call forth holy sentiments of love and admiration, in which that heart speaks to God and which are really as much a part of our nature as reason itself. Even the silent temple in the dim twilight, when no ceremony enlivens it, speaks to the soul and evokes its piety and its love of the beautiful!

"Hail, sacred tabernacles," cries Lamartine,[18] a child of genius speaking on this subject:

Hail, sacred tabernacles, where thou, O Lord, dost descend at the voice of a mortal. Hail, mysterious altar, where faith comes to receive its immortal food.

When the last hour has groaned in thy solemn towers; when its last beam fades away and dies in the dome; when the widow, holding her child by the hand, has wept on the pavement

[18] Alphonse de Lamartine (1790–1869).

and retraced her steps like a silent ghost; when the sigh of the distant organ seems lulled to rest with the day; when the nave is deserted, and the Levite, attentive to the lamps of the holy place, hardly crosses it again; then is the hour when I go to glide under thy obscure vault, and to seek, while nature sleeps, Him that ever watches.

Ye columns that veil the sacred asylums which my eyes dare not penetrate, at the foot of your immovable trunks I come to sigh. Forests of porphyry and marble! The air which the soul breathes under your arches is full of mystery and of peace.

Let love and anxious cares seek shade and solitude in the green shelter of groves to soothe their secret wounds.

O darkness of the sanctuary! The eye of religion prefers thee to the woods which the breezes disturb. Nothing changes thy foliage. Thy still shade is the image of motionless eternity.

Eternal pillars! Where are the hands that formed you? Man dies, but the holy thought animates the stone.

I love, O Lord, the obscurity of thy temple, inhabited alone by thee and by death. One hears from afar the flood of time, which roars on the borders of eternity.[19]

As real as reason is the power here appealed to. It is not a question of the slavery of reason but of the liberation and the sanctification of the sense of the beautiful. As real as reason is that love of the beautiful within the human soul.

Therefore, the Church, by appealing to this, does not silence reason, does not lead reason captive, but acts upon another power in the soul: she acts upon the heart without enslaving the intellect; she acts upon and sanctifies the imagination, sanctifies the love of the beautiful.

In her honor, be it said, that she possesses the greatest power to call forth these religious and sanctifying sentiments.

We use these arts in God's service, without enslaving the reason, for another reason. You go into

[19] Quoted in Kenelm Henry Digby, *Mores Catholici; or, Ages of Faith*, 11 vols. (London: J. Booker, 1831), 397.

a Catholic Church; you see a number of pictures around the wall; you see a number of people passing from picture to picture in procession. They are performing what is called the Stations of the Cross. They kneel before these pictures. Of course, they do not adore them. They show respect to the picture, on a principle similar to that by which you respect an oil painting of your dead father or mother. They are not so foolish as to suppose there is life or strength in these material objects. But they kneel before them, because they remind them of the sufferings of our divine Lord. In each picture is depicted a scene of His Passion.

You see the people moving in procession; you see old men mingling with little children. The old men can no longer read, but the Church holds before them the book of large pictures of the Stations of the Cross.

She has a catholicity of means of getting at the human soul, as she has a catholicity of doctrine. She has means, if one sense be closed, by which she tells the story of redemption through another.

They behold these scenes in the life of our divine Lord. They are instructed at once and moved to pity and to sorrow for sin. How often, too, have I seen little children looking at one of these Stations of the Cross, representing, perhaps, the nailing of the sacred hands of our Lord to the wood. There were the nails piercing and the great hammer lifted up; and I have seen in the eyes of the little children tears of sympathy—perhaps the first tears of sympathy they have ever shed. They have shed tears for their own sufferings, but it is not often that little children will weep at once for the sufferings of others.

I have often thought that perhaps the first sweet offering, the first crystal tear of sympathy, from the eyes of the little child was an offering to the bleeding heart of Jesus Christ in the Stations of the Cross.

How beautiful, how reasonable, how useful, are all those means of enlightening the intellect of man and of touching the heart of man!

"But why all the grandeur of your great cathedrals and their functions? Why all this pomp and show? Why not communicate directly, spirit to spirit?"

Because man is not purely a spirit. He has a body. There must be offered to God the tribute of the body in external worship.

Again, man cannot, while he remains on this earth, keep in constant union with the Divinity without external aids. God Himself, in the magnificent temple of creation, gives us evidence that He rejected not the beautiful in preparing this temple for His own service.

Look at it in all its splendor, for He created it, as the Apostle says, "that the invisible things of Him, from the beginning of the world, be clearly seen, being understood by the things that are visible, His eternal power also and His divinity."[20] Has God rejected the beautiful in this temple of creation?

Who was it, when He formed this temple, that first introduced into it sculpture, painting, poetry, music — those marvelous missionaries of the beautiful that, like the angels in the vision of sleeping Israel, bring earth and heaven into sweet union?

Who was the first sculptor that struck with his chisel the marble rocks and fashioned them as He would?

Who was the first painter that touched with His brush the flowers of the valley and tinged with deep

---

[20] Rom. 1:20, Douay-Rheims.

azure the ocean — that mystic baptismal font in whose waters He purified the universe, and decreed that by its waters and His spirit, man should become regenerate?

Who was the first inspirer of music?

Who was the first decorator, who studded with gems the Milky Way and spread this arch of splendor across the concave of this His temple?

Who first told the strong sons of God to "shout with joy,"[21] and bade "the morning stars sing together,"[22] when all creation was ringing with the notes of Him; the first composer when earth and air and heaven celebrated His praises until the intruder sin broke the universal chorus, jarred against nature's chime, tore the harp strings of His angels, and who, by conquering sin and death, brings back the lost melody?

Who has sanctified this art of music? Not to oppress the intellect, not to cloud it, not to silence it, not to lull it into a sleep fatal to its powers — no, but to beautify, to elevate, and to influence even the intellect itself, by purifying the imagination and the heart.

[21] Isaiah 44:23.
[22] Cf. Job 38:7

He it was who, having inspired this glorious art, declared that music should become in heaven itself eternal; that when all the other arts should, as it were, faint at the gates of Heaven, when the chisel should fall from the sculptor's hand on seeing the magnificent ideals that he thought to represent; when the painter should cast away the brush in view of the glorious coloring beyond the stars; when the poet should breathe no more the song of hope, but should enjoy eternal fruition; when the architect need no more to build a house with hands in view of the eternal temple of Almighty God; when the sacred mission of all the other arts shall have been fulfilled, that then glorious music should survive them all, and flying in, as it were, through the gates of light, give her lessons to the angels, and the architect and the sculptor and the painter and the poet should all become for eternity the children of song.[23]

[23] The arts appeared also in God's Temple of Jerusalem (1 Kings 7–8), where, for instance, the sculptured cherubim adorned the Ark and men bowed down before it — but not in adoration of it — precisely as Catholics act in our temples.

In all of this, where is the slavery of the intellect?

Hence, that man at St. Peter's should not have risen from his position, should not have broken the enchanting bonds, but should have said to himself: "This Church has won my heart—has touched it in religious worship, as it was never touched before. I shall consider whether this Church which is so beautiful, this Church which moves the depths of the human soul so marvelously, may not also satisfy my intellect, and thus it will have won at once both powers."

Thus acted the distinguished American citizen Judge Burnett, former governor of California and the author of that admirable book *The Path Which Led a Protestant Lawyer to the Catholic Church*.[24] He had been present at Christmas midnight Mass. He had felt his heart moved in a manner, as he himself said, that he had never experienced before. He did not become a Catholic *because* he was so influenced, as that would

[24] Peter H. Burnett, *The Path Which Led a Protestant Law-yer to the Catholic Church* (New York: D. Appleton, 1860).

be illogical; but he continued to examine, and when his intellect was convinced, after his heart was moved, he bowed that intellect—and it is a noble one—he bowed both intellect and heart to the influence of the truth and beauty of the Catholic Church.

In this there is nothing illogical or degrading. Hence there is no slavery in the Church's use of ceremonies, in the Church's use of the arts in her worship of God, as means that will bring the soul nearer to God and are in harmony with certain powers of the soul herself. And what can be more appropriate than to offer the tribute of all that is beautiful in nature and art at the footstool of the throne of the God of the beautiful! Whatever brings the soul nearer to God, in such a manner as to be affected by the influence of God on its powers, is to be embraced, is to be used.

Nor is there danger of idolatry in all this. No man is absurd enough to suppose that in the use of these statues and pictures, we will regard them as deities. The thing is too absurd. Indeed, it is beginning to be regarded as absurd by the most intelligent Protestants of the day, who very freely, I think, understand that in the use of these objects of worship there is little or no fear of our being so ridiculous as to mistake them for deities!

The Church does not wrongly promote love of Mary and the saints.

The Church does not degrade religion by placing any creature on the throne of God. God alone she adores. Catholics do not believe that the Blessed Virgin, or any saint, or all the saints together, can receive anything like the slightest act of adoration. Adoration is due to God alone. "The Lord thy God shalt thou adore."[25] It would be high treason against the King of Kings to place anyone on His throne.

[25] Matt. 4:10.

Between God and the first archangel of heaven —between God and that sweet Virgin Mary, who was so near to Him in life, there must be (in the sense of divinity) an infinite distance, because the Divinity is infinitely above all His creatures.

The Blessed Virgin and the saints are but the works of His hands. He is the infinite and eternal God, and no Catholic believes that any of these creatures should be worshipped as the infinite and eternal God is worshipped. All that they have, they have received from Him. They shine by His reflected light. He is a jealous God. He will not give His glory to another.

True: but He cannot be jealous of these creatures of His, no matter how exalted they may be, as these creatures acknowledge Him and we confess that all that they have must come from him.

Can you imagine an artist jealous of his own picture—a picture that he himself has executed? Suppose you are praising the picture. Can you imagine the artist coming to you and saying: "Don't praise the picture; praise me"? Would you not say, "Why, sir, I am praising you in your picture"?

Can you imagine an author jealous of his own book? And if persons praise it, is it any derogation from the praise due to him?

Can you imagine an architect jealous of the stately building that he himself has designed?

No. You would say this is mere folly indeed. Neither can God be jealous of any honor given to these creatures, *as creatures*. They are the books of which He is the author; they are the paintings, as it were, of which He is the artist; they are the splendid buildings of which He is the architect; and, therefore, there is no degradation of religion, no placing of any creature whatever in the place of God, because, between Him and the highest creature there is this infinite distance.

And, therefore, the charge falls to the ground when we know that Catholics do not believe that the Blessed Virgin ought to be worshipped as if she were a goddess; when we know that Catholics do not believe that any honor can be given to her or to any saint, independently of the Deity and that all the glory they have is but the reflected glory of the most high God.

Let us suppose for a moment, as someone has suggested, that after Washington had achieved the liberties of the American people, he comes forward upon the platform before them. They are cheering him, their deliverer; and let us suppose that Washington's mother comes out on the platform, and someone says: "Let us cheer the mother who gave us such a son."

Do you think Washington would be jealous of the honor given to his own mother, and given to her chiefly *because* she was his mother, because of him?

And wherefore shall our divine Lord be jealous of the honor given to His Mother when that honor is given especially because she was His Mother?

"But you pray so long to the Blessed Virgin and to the saints, and sometimes pray but for a short time to Almighty God. Is not this evidence that you are thinking more of these creatures of God than you are of God Himself?"

It is not the length of time that we spend praying that determines the character of the prayer. One bending of the knee in adoration, which must be offered to God alone, is a higher act of worship than if one were a century praying without adoration.

If the Catholic performs acts of worship that mislead the non-Catholic — long prayers or bowing before statues of the Blessed Virgin or swinging the censers before the statues of saints or angels — you must remember that the character of the worship is to be judged by the doctrine, not the doctrine by the worship.

You must have first the key to what the Catholic means by these external expressions, either in action or in word, before you understand, and certainly before you condemn, this external action. I may bow the knee without intending adoration.

In the old English Book of Common Prayer, in the Protestant marriage service, the bridegroom uses the words, if I remember rightly: "With this ring I thee wed, and with my body I thee worship."

Now, if someone said to him, "Do you really mean to adore this creature? You say you worship her."

"Oh, no," he will say. "You must first understand what I mean by *worship*. Words are words. It is the meaning attached to the word, and it is by that meaning I have to be judged. I honor her. It does not mean here such worship as you imagine."

In earlier times, in the religious sense of the term, men adored, as the term implies, by placing the hand to the mouth, and then toward the statue — *ad os*, "to the mouth." So kissing hands was supreme adoration. It is not now, of course, supreme adoration.

The external act, then, must be interpreted by the internal intention, and the internal intention by the *teaching of the Church* on the subject.

There is no Catholic who believes that it would not be idolatry and blasphemy to offer to any being that supreme worship that is due to God alone; and hence he cannot have any intention of adoration in these otherwise indifferent acts.

He may indeed spend a long time in asking the saints or the Blessed Virgin to pray for him, but he well knows it is only God who can bestow on him what he wants. If a man who desires an office from the president knows that it is only the president who can give it but may spend a long time in conversation with some dear friend of the president, you do not conclude from this that he thinks this friend can do more for him than the president can! He is only encouraging the friend to go to the president to ask the favor for him.[26] So Catholics ask the saints to pray for them, as non-Catholics ask *one another's prayers.*

Thus, when you know what Catholics really do believe on these subjects, you will find no difficulty in understanding how rational that faith is, and how far from degrading.

"But here," says another, "are inanimate objects. These inanimate objects are honored in the same manner, and are even said to perform miracles. Now, if inanimate objects perform miracles, there must be divinity in these inanimate objects. Therefore, you deify the object.

"You suppose that in that old bone of a saint, or in that old crucifix, there is a power to perform miracles, and here is surely idolatry. Here is certainly a derogation from the honor that should be given to Almighty God; and here it is worse than in the case

[26] It is in this intercessory sense that we call the Blessed Virgin our hope and other such affectionate names. Here is the key to all the apparently extravagant terms used in addressing her. And surely if we ask fellow sinners on earth to pray for us without degrading religion, we may ask saints in heaven.

of the Blessed Virgin or the saints, because they are rational and holy beings, but here is an inanimate, vile object of the earth, to which you attribute the power of performing miracles."

Miracles are perpetually performed, it is said, by these objects in the hands of saints, and a great many stories, sometimes very amusing ones, are told of the number and manner and marvelous character of these miracles. I will relate to you a few of these pious stories and then proceed to illustrate the subject.

Once there was a pious, credulous people, and in their country there lived an old saint in a hermitage, near the banks of a lake, apart from the world, with only one lay brother. One day this saint took a walk by the bank of the lake. He saw a woodman felling trees. The hatchet of the poor man fell into the lake, and the saint, with a marvelous facility for performing miracles by the aid of inanimate objects, took a little twig from a tree, coaxed the hatchet up, and gave it to the woodman, who went on his way rejoicing.

The saint returned home and found there a poor widow who had come with the request that he should go and raise her child to life. She supposed he could do anything that he pleased.

The saint was probably fatigued after his walk, and didn't wish to go, so he called to the lay brother and said, "Brother, take this walking stick of mine, and with it revive this poor woman's child."

After a while the saint died—for saints will die, too—and they buried him. In the open grave of the saint another body was subsequently placed.

The saint, who was very fond of solitude during his life, rather rejoiced in it after death and didn't want this man in the same grave with him. Therefore, with the same facility for performing miracles, his inanimate body brought the man to life without being restored to life itself and sent him on his way rejoicing.

Now, in the same country, there lived another saint, and as the people were grievously affected by snakes, this saint, who was not as cruel to the snakes as a certain Irish saint who expelled them all, erected a large cross, something like the mission cross that you may see outside or inside of certain churches, and told the people that, when they were bitten by the snakes, they should look at the cross, and they would be cured; and it is said that they were.

This saint had a box made, in which he placed some relics and told the people that they must take great care of the box, that it would always protect them, and, when they went to fight, they must bear it with them. Their enemies, however, got hold of the box on one occasion, but they were soon very glad to return it to these simple, good people, as it tormented them.

And there lived among them later on another saint who performed miracles, not merely by the use of inanimate, senseless objects like these, but when he was performing miracles in one direction, his shadow was performing them in the other.

Now, in what chronicle of the Middle Ages, in what old monkish *Lives of Saints*, have I found the account of these saints performing miracles by the aid of these inanimate objects?

Where have I found these accounts? Substantially in the Protestant *Bible*, and, of course, in the Catholic Bible, too.

Elisha, the prophet, was walking by the banks of a river; a man was felling trees and the axe fell into the water. The prophet, by the aid of the little twig, brought up the iron till it swam upon the surface, and he then returned it to the grateful woodman.[27]

There was a widow whose only child was dead, and Elisha did not go at first to raise the child, but called his man and said, "Take my staff" — which, after all, was his walking stick — "and lay it upon the face of the child."[28]

Elisha was also the inhospitable buried saint whose dead bones (relics) restored the intruder to life.[29]

But who was the saint who erected the large cross to protect the people from the biting of the snakes? Who but Moses, who erected the brazen serpent that was to symbolize the Cross and told the people when bitten by the serpents to look at that brazen serpent and they would be healed?[30]

And what was the box of relics but the ark of the covenant, with the rod of Aaron, with the vessel of

[27] 2 Kings 6:5–6.
[28] 2 Kings 4:28–37.
[29] 2 Kings 13:21.
[30] Numbers 21:9.

manna, with the tables of the law, with those venerable relics — all inanimate objects![31]

And who was the saint whose shadow (not even an inanimate object) performed miracles, but St. Peter? For we are told in the Acts of the Apostles that people brought their sick that his shadow might fall upon them.[32]

So the Catholic believes nothing in regard to these subjects substantially different from what is contained in the *Bible* — which the Protestant must also accept.

Nor can even the rationalist object if he admits the existence of God and His angels. God could use inanimate objects as He uses animate objects. What is the difference to Him between the first spirit in heaven and the humblest inanimate object on earth? Both being creatures must be infinitely beneath Him. It is only a question of the difference between *two little things*.

Therefore, there is nothing irrational in supposing that God, for His own ends (which sometimes are patent and sometimes concealed) can act through

[31] Exodus 40.
[32] Acts 5:15.

these external objects. These relics do not perform the miracles. God acts through them. God uses them, just as He uses men; there is no divinity in them. God uses them simply as an instrument.

Surely God can do just as He pleases with His own creatures, in the manner that He pleases, when He pleases, and no man dare ask Him why.

I may add, in passing, when we hear of those marvelous things, of miracles and visions and so forth, the Catholic does not believe that he is bound to accept them all.

What! Every imagination of every excitable person; every vision of every intensified, highly wrought mind!

No! These reported miracles have to be examined on the very same laws of evidence by which any other facts are examined. I examine the reported fact; I bring to it the ordinary laws of evidence; I reject or accept it on evidence brought before me, admitting, of course, the *possibility* of Almighty God's having performed a miracle—the possibility but not the fact, until it shall have been proved. Hence there is no degradation of either reason or religion.

Catholic priests do not perform deeds reserved for God alone.

Neither is it true that the Church tends to demoralize the individual or the national conscience by her use of the power that God gave His apostles on the very day of His Resurrection when He said: "If you forgive the sins of any, they are forgiven" (John 20:23).

The confessor is simply God's agent, and just as the clergyman who baptizes the child washes away the Original Sin that was on the soul of the child—just as the Protestant clergyman or the layman or whoever baptizes the child washes away this Original Sin from the soul of the child, doing it as God's agent — so the priest forgives the actual sin, but only as God's agent. The power given to him is a delegated power; he cannot exercise it beyond the limits assigned by Him who delegated it.

Now, Almighty God will not forgive a man's sins without sorrow for them, necessary reparation for their effects, and a determination to enter on a new life. The priest can never forgive the sins of a man who is not truly contrite. The priest has no power over such a soul. If the priest had this tremendous power to forgive sins as he pleased, then the confessional should be abolished in every civilized country. Then it would demoralize any people on the face of God's earth; then it would indeed lessen man's horror of sin.

The absurd, the blasphemous position that a man could do what the eternal God Himself will not do — forgive the sins of a man who is not sorry for them, who will not amend his life and make reparation to property or character for injury done; to suppose this would be, indeed, to suppose all that is popularly supposed by Protestants as held in the Catholic doctrine of confession.

Nor is there any fatal facility in obtaining pardon, because the Catholic, in order to obtain pardon, has to do *all that the Protestant has to do* before he goes to confession at all. He must be sorry for his sin; he must purpose amendment; he must go through all these preparations of the soul in order to fit himself to go to confession. Hence there is no fatal facility, no lessening of the horror due to sin; and these dispositions are required from everyone who goes to confession.

The discipline is universal.

Look at that old man, over eighty-five years of age, moving toward that barefoot monk in the confessional. This old man kneels down before the monk, and says: "Bless me, Father, for I have sinned. I confess to Almighty God that I have sinned, through my fault, through my fault, through my most grievous fault." He tells his sins, and the priest must be certain that he is sorry for them.

Who is this old man, thus humbled? Who is this man who falls at the feet of the poor monk?

Pope Pius IX himself!

He has to go to confession; he has to be sorry for his sins, and the priest would be bound, at the peril of his eternal salvation, to send even him away from the tribunal, unless—if you can imagine such a thing—he were not certain that he had the necessary dispositions.

Wonderful Church, which, while it exalts the office, ever humbles the man![33]

This discipline is universal, and therefore the individual conscience is not demoralized by this practice, and, by consequence, neither is the conscience of a people.

Hear the testimony of a man as to the effect of the confessional, not only on the individual soul, but on the nation also. Hear one who is unexceptional as such a witness, who entertained the deepest and most intense hatred of religion that ever burned in an infidel heart; but who knew, from his own experience when he used to go to confession, and when, perhaps, he was pure and good, the value of the confessional upon his soul. This witness is Voltaire himself.[34] He says:

[33] From this it follows that we Catholics do not believe that papal infallibility involves papal impeccability.

[34] Voltaire (1694–1778)

There is no wiser institution than that of con-fession. The most of mankind, guilty of crimes, are naturally tormented with remorse. The law-givers who established mysteries and expiations, were equally anxious to prevent the criminals, under the influence of despair, from rushing recklessly into new crimes.

Confession is an excellent thing—a bridle on inveterate crimes. It is excellent for dispos-ing hearts, ulcerated with hatred, to forgive, and the unjust to repair the injuries they may have done to their neighbor.

The enemies of the Roman Church, who oppose so salutary an institution, have taken away from man the greatest check that can be imagined on iniquity. The wise men of antiq-uity have all recognized its importance.[35]

Leibniz,[36] one of the greatest men that Protestant-ism or any other *ism* can boast of—the equal of Sir

[35] Voltaire (1694–1778), *Oeuvres Complètes de Voltaire*, 4 vols. (Paris: Leroi É. Féret, 1833), 1:550.

[36] Gottfried Wilhelm (von) Leibniz (1646–1716).

Isaac Newton in physical science and his superior in almost every other department—speaks of confession in terms that might be employed by the most devoted frequenter of the sacred tribunal.

If Catholic nations seem sometimes morally degraded, depend on it that the immoral people who bring disgrace on them are not the people who go to confession but often the infidel radicals who denounce it. Left under its sacred influence, they would be very different indeed if they lamented before God their sins and received the salutary counsel that they cannot receive until they have resolved to become new creatures.

Conclusion

✛

Therefore, these charges fall to the ground for these reasons:

- A Catholic does not submit his intellect to a human institution in order to find out the truth of God, but submits it to what he has convinced himself is a divine institution.
- Catholics do not believe, and the Church does not teach, that the Scriptures should be kept from the people.
- Catholics do not believe that in ceremonies and in external pomp and show, and in the use of the arts, that in these alone there is religion, but that they have to be used as aids to bring the soul into communion with God, who has to be worshipped "in spirit and in truth."

- Catholics do not believe that the creature has to take the place of the Creator.
- Catholics do not worship pictures or images as if they are deities and give supreme worship to anyone but to God alone.
- There is no fatal facility in obtaining pardon for sin and no degrading influence, but a marvelous conservatism in the use of the confessional.

Therefore is it true that:
- The Church does not enslave the intellect.
- The Church does not degrade religion.
- The Church does not demoralize the people.

In order that you may be confirmed in the truth of what I have said to you, no matter what may have been your opinions before, let me read to you a short summary of points of doctrine that we Catholics condemn and anathematize. In a little work that has been extensively circulated in England, Ireland, and this country, these points are summarized in a striking manner.

Any Catholic can, with his hand on the Bible and in a solemn oath, say, "Amen" to the following propositions:

- Cursed is he who commits idolatry, who prays to images or relics, or worships them for God. Amen.
- Cursed is every goddess worshipper who believes the Virgin Mary to be any more than a creature, who worships her or puts his trust in her more than in God; who believes her above her Son, or that she can in any way command Him. Amen.
- Cursed is he who believes the saints in heaven to be his redeemers, who prays to them as such, or who gives God's honor to them or to any creature whatsoever.
- Cursed is he who believes that priests can forgive sins, whether the sinner repent or not, or that there is any power on earth that can forgive sin without a hearty repentance and a serious amendment.
- Cursed is he who believes that there is authority in the pope or in any other person

that can give leave to commit sin or that for a sum of money can forgive sins.

- Cursed is he who believes that, independently of the merits and Passion of Christ, he can obtain salvation by his own works or make condign satisfaction for the guilt of his sins or the eternal pains due to them.

- Cursed is he who condemns the Word of God or who hides it from the people in order to keep them from a knowledge of their duty and to preserve them in ignorance and error.

- Cursed is he who undervalues the Word of God, or that, forsaking the Scripture, chooses rather to follow human traditions than it.

- Cursed is he who believes that the pope can give to any, on any occasion whatsoever, dispensations to lie or swear falsely, or that it is lawful for any at the last hour to protest himself innocent in case he is guilty.

- Cursed is he who teaches it to be lawful to do anything wicked, though it be for the interest and good of "Mother Church," or that any evil action may be done that good may come from it. Amen.

- Finally, cursed are we if, in answering or in saying, "Amen" to any of these curses, we use any equivocation or mental reservation, or do not assent to them in the common and obvious sense of the terms. Amen.

Can Catholics, then, seriously and without check of conscience say, "Amen" to all these curses? Yes, they can, and they are ready to do so whenever and as often as it shall be required of them.

Here is the evidence of what Catholics *do not* believe, for the first time perhaps understood by many generous-hearted people here tonight — people who have felt that they would not do injustice or wrong to any individual and who will not do injustice anymore to hundreds of millions of individuals on God's earth.

But that injustice has been done, and therefore is it essential that it should be undone, as far as each individual who hears me is concerned. Millions of people demand reparation, because the very doctrines that they curse are the doctrines that they have been falsely charged with believing. These are the doctrines Catholics *do not* believe.

The Church could never have lasted under the weight of all the persecutions and misrepresentations of this kind if she were not the Church of the living God — if she had not the promise that the "gates of hell should not prevail against her."[37]

That is the promise that sustains her, directs her, and inspires her — that has been her guarantee of triumph for over eighteen hundred years and shall be until the end.

[37] Matt. 16:18.

Postscript

✠

Never shall I forget the evidences that I once saw and heard of the stability of this Church in her war against the powers of hell, of which one is this very misrepresentation of which I have been complaining.

It was in Rome in 1867. On that occasion, the eighteen hundredth anniversary of the death of St. Peter, we were assembled in the magnificent basilica that bears his name. Five hundred bishops gathered around the sovereign pontiff—bishops from every tribe and nation on earth. There he stood, the Supreme Pontiff, the great central figure. Forty thousand wax lights illumined the magnificent assembly. The sculptured saints of eighteen centuries looked down upon us from their niches and from the tombs around. The vast basilica was crowded to its utmost capacity.

The papal choir, near the grand altar, commenced to sing these words, "Thou art Peter, and upon this rock I will build my Church,"[38] and when these one hundred voices seemed to have exhausted all their power and beauty of melody, three hundred voices above the entrance to St. Peter's continued the text, "I will build my Church," and the two choirs united, and then four hundred voices—the *Chorus Angelo-rum*—in the dome, "that vast and wondrous dome to which Diana's marvel was a cell,"[39] continued this text, and in the end the basso voices commencing, and the whole magnificent ocean of melody surging onward, they sang, "And the gates of hell shall not prevail against it—*Portae inferi, non prevalebunt.*"

We heard the *non* at the altar; we heard it above the distant portals; we heard it ringing around and around the dome. That text sounded in my mind that day as the announcement of a fact—of a challenge—of a prophecy. There, above the tomb of Peter; there,

[38] Matt.16:18.
[39] George Gordon, Lord Byron, "Childe Harold," canto 153.

where opposing powers had met for eighteen hundred years; there, where they had measured lances, these powers of hell and the old, united Church — the misrepresented, but still glorious Church — these words sounded like the announcement of the fact that after eighteen hundred years of fighting, she was still victorious.

They rang out like a challenge, as if she said, "Come forth and fight the battle for eighteen centuries more if you wish it" and like a prophecy that that battle should end victoriously for her because of God's great promise!

O glorious Church of the living God!

O only divine institution upon earth!

In all thy power, in all thy unity, in all thy beauty, calumniated but not less lovely, here is the sanction for thy continuance, here the communicated life of God that gives thee vitality and which will crown thee with victory for evermore.

> *"On this rock I will build my church.*
> *The gates of hell shall not prevail against it."*

Bibliography

Burnett, Peter H. *The Path Which Led a Protestant Lawyer to the Catholic Church*. New York: D. Appleton, 1860.

Digby, Kenelm Henry. *Mores Catholici; or, Ages of Faith*. 11 vols. London: J. Booker, 1831.

Guizot, François. *General History of Civilization in Europe: From the Fall of the Roman Empire to the French Revolution*. 2nd American ed. New York: D. Appleton, 1840.

Macaulay, Thomas Babington. *Critical and Historical Essays Contributed to the Edinburgh Review*. 6th ed. 3 vols. London: Longman, Brown, Green, and Longmans, 1849.

Voltaire. *Oeuvres Complètes de Voltaire*. 4 vols. Paris: Leroi É. Féret, 1833.

Patrick John Ryan
(1831–1911)

✠

Born in County Tipperary, Ireland, Patrick John Ryan was ordained there as a subdeacon in 1852, the same year he left England for the United States, where he became attached to the Archdiocese of St. Louis in Missouri.

Ordained the following year, he soon became rector of the cathedral of St. Louis. In 1872 he was appointed coadjutor archbishop of St. Louis, and in 1884 became the second archbishop of Philadelphia.

In his twenty-seven-year tenure there, Archbishop Ryan erected 170 churches and 82 schools, increased the number of priests by 322 and nuns by 1,545, and saw the Catholic population almost double to 525,000 souls. In addition, he established homes for orphans while doubling the capacity of the city's three Catholic hospitals. He died just nine days before his eightieth birthday.

Sophia Institute

Sophia Institute is a nonprofit institution that seeks to nurture the spiritual, moral, and cultural life of souls and to spread the Gospel of Christ in conformity with the authentic teachings of the Roman Catholic Church.

Sophia Institute Press fulfills this mission by offering translations, reprints, and new publications that afford readers a rich source of the enduring wisdom of mankind.

Sophia Institute also operates two popular online Catholic resources: CrisisMagazine.com and CatholicExchange.com.

Crisis Magazine provides insightful cultural analysis that arms readers with the arguments necessary for navigating the ideological and theological minefields of the day. *Catholic Exchange* provides world news from a Catholic perspective as well as daily devotionals and articles that will help you to grow in holiness and live a life consistent with the teachings of the Church.

In 2013, Sophia Institute launched Sophia Institute for Teachers to renew and rebuild Catholic culture through service to Catholic education. With the goal of nurturing the spiritual, moral, and cultural life of souls, and an abiding respect for the role and work of teachers, we strive to provide materials and programs that are at once enlightening to the mind and ennobling to the heart; faithful and complete, as well as useful and practical.

Sophia Institute gratefully recognizes the Solidarity Association for preserving and encouraging the growth of our apostolate over the course of many years. Without their generous and timely support, this book would not be in your hands.

www.SophiaInstitute.com
www.CatholicExchange.com
www.CrisisMagazine.com
www.SophiaInstituteforTeachers.org